# SACREDSPACE

## for Lent 2008

*Gladys Compié*

# SACREDSPACE

## for Lent 2008

from the web site www.sacredspace.ie

Jesuit Communication Centre, Ireland

ave maria press AMP notre dame, indiana

# Acknowledgment

The publisher would like to thank Alan McGuckian, S.J., Gerry Bourke, S.J., and Piaras Jackson, S.J., for their kind assistance in making this book possible. Correspondence with the Sacred Space team can be directed to feedback@sacredspace.ie. Piaras Jackson, S.J., Gerry Bourke, S.J., Paul Andrews, S.J., and John McDermott welcome all comments on the material or on the site.

Unless otherwise noted, the Scripture quotations contained herein are from the *New Revised Standard Version Bible*, copyright © 1989 by the Division of Christian Education of the National Council of the Churches of Christ in the United States of America. Used by permission. All rights reserved.

Published under license from Michelle Anderson Publishing Pty. Ltd. in Australia.

Founded in 1865, Ave Maria Press is a ministry of the Indiana Province of Holy Cross.

www.avemariapress.com

ISBN-10: 1-59471-160-7   ISBN-13: 978-1-59471-160-2

Cover and text design by K.H. Coney.

Printed and bound in the United States of America.

# how to use this book

During this Lenten season, we invite you to make a sacred space in your day. Spend ten minutes praying here and now, wherever you are, with the help of a prayer guide and scripture chosen specially for each day. Every place is a sacred space so you may wish to have this little book available at any time or place during the course of the day . . . in your desk at work, while traveling, on your bedside table, in your purse or jacket pocket. . . . Remember that God is everywhere, all around us, constantly reaching out to us, even in the most unlikely situations. When we know this, and with a bit of practice, we can pray anywhere.

The following pages will guide you through a session of prayer stages.

Something to think and pray about each day
   this week

The Presence of God

Freedom

Consciousness

The Word (leads you to the daily Lenten scripture and provides help with the text)

Conversation

Conclusion

It is most important to come back to these pages each day of the week as they are an integral
part of each day's prayer and lead to the scripture and inspiration points.

   Although written in the first person, the
prayers are for "doing" rather than for reading
out. Each stage is a kind of exercise or media-
tion aimed at helping you to get in touch with
God and God's presence in your life.

We hope that you will join the many people around the world praying with us in our sacred space.

# The Presence of God

Bless all who worship you, almighty God,
from the rising of the sun to its setting:
from your goodness enrich us,
by your love inspire us,
by your Spirit guide us,
by your power protect us,
in your mercy receive us,
now and always.

# february 6–9

Something to think and pray about each day this week:

## Getting Started

We are starting Lent this week, a somber time.

You did not come, O God, to judge us, but to seek what is lost, to set free those who are imprisoned in guilt and fear, and to save us when our hearts accuse us. Take us as we are, with all that sinful past of the world. You are greater than our hearts, and greater than all our guilt—you are the creator of a new future and a God of Love forever and ever.

## The Presence of God

At any time of the day or night
we can call on Jesus.
He is always waiting,
listening for our call.
What a wonderful blessing!
No phone needed, no e-mails,
just a whisper.

## Freedom

I will ask God's help,
to be free from my own preoccupations,
to be open to God in this time of prayer,
to come to love and serve him more.

## Consciousness

How am I really feeling?
Light-hearted? Heavy-hearted?
I may be very much at peace,
happy to be here.

Equally, I may be frustrated,
worried or angry.
I acknowledge how I really am.
It is the real me that the Lord loves.

## The Word

I read the word of God slowly, a few times
over, and I listen to what God is saying to me.
(Please turn to your scripture on the following
pages. Inspiration points are there should you
need them. When you are ready, return here
to continue.)

## Conversation

Remembering that I am
still in God's presence,
I imagine Jesus himself sitting beside me,
and say whatever is on my mind,
whatever is in my heart,
speaking as one friend to another.

## Conclusion

Glory be to the Father, and to the Son, and to the Holy Spirit, as it was in the beginning, is now and ever shall be, world without end. Amen.

## Wednesday 6th February,
## Ash Wednesday        Matthew 6:1–4

Jesus said to his disciples, "So whenever you give alms, do not sound a trumpet before you, as the hypocrites do in the synagogues and in the streets, so that they may be praised by others. Truly I tell you, they have received their reward. But when you give alms, do not let your left hand know what your right hand is doing, so that your alms may be done in secret; and your Father who sees in secret will reward you."

- The forty days of Lent recall the desert where the people of Israel, and then John the Baptist, and then Jesus himself, made their journey to a new life. The desert was not a destination, but a place for travelers going somewhere. In our liturgy that somewhere is Easter, the feast of the risen Lord.

- In each of our lives, Lent can be more than that; it can be the start of a second journey. It is a time to tame our appetites for food, sex, drink, sleep, or whatever has too much of a hold on us. It is a time to regain our freedom.

**Thursday 7th February          Luke 9:22–25**

Jesus said to his disciples: "The Son of Man must undergo great suffering, and be rejected by the elders, chief priests, and scribes, and be killed, and on the third day be raised." Then he said to them all, "If any want to become my followers, let them deny themselves and take up their cross daily and follow me. For those who want to save their life will lose it, and those who lose their life for my sake will save it. What does it profit them if they gain the whole world, but lose or forfeit themselves?"

- Deny yourself and take up your cross daily. Lord, I used to think this meant looking for mortifications. You have taught me that my cross is myself, my ego, the pains in my body, my awkwardness, my mistakes.

- To follow you is to move beyond ego-trips. It means coping with the business of life without trampling on others or making them suffer. There is a world here to be explored this Lent.

## Friday 8th February ✝     Isaiah 58:5–9

Is such the fast that I choose, a day to humble oneself? Is it to bow down the head like a bulrush, and to lie in sackcloth and ashes? Will you call this a fast, a day acceptable to the Lord? Is not this the fast that I choose: to loose the bonds of injustice, to undo the thongs of the yoke, to let the oppressed go free, and to break every yoke? Is it not to share your bread with the hungry, and bring the homeless poor into your house; when you see the naked, to cover them, and not to hide yourself from your own kin? Then your light shall break forth like the dawn, and your healing shall spring up quickly; your vindicator shall go before you, the glory of the Lord shall be your rear guard. Then you shall call, and the Lord will answer; you shall cry for help, and he will say, Here I am.

- "Loosing the bonds of injustice, undoing the thongs of the yoke and letting the oppressed go free." All around me there are people suffering from unfairness; they may be children, old people, immigrants, each unable to raise their voice in protest. ✝

- Lord, you are inviting me to have an eye for injustice, and take a stand against it, or at least never connive with it. Give my heart a habit of justice, restless when faced with what is unfair.

**Saturday 9th February**  **Luke 5:27–32**

After this he went out and saw a tax collector named Levi, sitting at the tax booth; and he said to him, "Follow me." And he got up, left everything, and followed him. Then Levi gave a great banquet for him in his house; and there was a large crowd of tax collectors and others sitting at the table with them. The Pharisees and their scribes were complaining to his disciples, saying, "Why do you eat and drink with tax collectors and sinners?" Jesus answered, "Those who are well have no need of a physician, but those who are sick; I have come to call not the righteous but sinners to repentance."

- Where are the Levis in my world? The drug-pushers, pedophiles, wife-batterers, rapists, those who cheat on tax or social welfare, those who are headlined for hatred in the tabloid press.

- Lord, these are the sick who need you as physician. Can I help you to reach out to them?

Something to think and pray about each day this week:

## Growing Pains

Lent reflects the rhythm of our spiritual life, between Tabor and Gethsemani, the Transfiguration and the Agony in the Garden. There are times when God shows himself, as on Tabor: prayer is easy, our hearts are light. We feel loved and loving, on holy ground. J.D. Salinger wrote: "All we do our whole lives is go from one little piece of holy ground to the next."

Then there are times of disagreeable growth. You remember the parable of the barren fig-tree (Luke 13:6), and the farmer who said: "I need a year to dig around it and manure it." We can feel God doing this to us, feel the pain when our roots are struck by the spade. We feel useless, past our best, no good to anyone, a failure in the most important things we have tried, whether marriage, vocation, rearing children, or our job and career. Life loses its savor. We cannot pray. We sense that some people think the world would be better off without us.

St. Ignatius called this state desolation, and he advised: "Remember that it will pass . . . In consolation, think about how you will conduct yourself in time of desolation. And insist more on prayer." Then you come to see—gradually—that this same ground, however stinking, is holy, and you can find God there. He is wielding the spade, spreading the dung.

## The Presence of God

For a few moments, I think of
God's veiled presence in things:
in the elements, giving them existence;
in plants, giving them life;
in animals, giving them sensation;
and finally, in me, giving me
all this and more, making me a temple,
a dwelling-place of the Spirit.

## Freedom

God is not foreign to my freedom.
Instead the Spirit breathes life
into my most intimate desires,
gently nudging me toward all that is good.
I ask for the grace to let myself
be enfolded by the Spirit.

## Consciousness

Knowing that God loves me unconditionally,
I can afford to be honest about how I am.

How has the last day been,
and how do I feel now?
I share my feelings openly with the Lord.

## The Word

The word of God comes down to us through
the scriptures. May the Holy Spirit enlighten
my mind and my heart to respond to the gospel
teachings. (Please turn to your scripture on the
following pages. Inspiration points are there
should you need them. When you are ready,
return here to continue.)

## Conversation

How has God's word moved me?
Has it left me cold?
Has it consoled me,
or moved me to act in a new way?
I imagine Jesus sitting beside me,
I turn and share my feelings with him.

## Conclusion

Glory be to the Father, and to the Son, and to the Holy Spirit, as it was in the beginning, is now and ever shall be, world without end. Amen.

## Sunday 10th February,
### First Sunday of Lent          Matthew 4:1–4

Then Jesus was led up by the Spirit into the wilderness to be tempted by the devil. He fasted forty days and forty nights, and afterwards he was famished. The tempter came and said to him, "If you are the Son of God, command these stones to become loaves of bread." But he answered, "It is written, 'One does not live by bread alone, but by every word that comes from the mouth of God.'"

- I too have known times of temptation when I felt on my own except for irrational forces that were messing up my life. Lord, you felt the influence of evil, and were tested. You were purified as you came through a difficult time.

- When I was in the middle of such a time, it did not feel like God's hand, but like desolation and despair. When I look back, I can see how God was shaping me.

**Monday 11th February  Matthew 25:31–40**

"When the Son of Man comes in his glory, and all the angels with him, then he will sit on the throne of his glory. All the nations will be gathered before him, and he will separate people one from another as a shepherd separates the sheep from the goats, and he will put the sheep at his right hand and the goats at the left. Then the king will say to those at his right hand, 'Come, you that are blessed by my Father, inherit the kingdom prepared for you from the foundation of the world; for I was hungry and you gave me food, I was thirsty and you gave me something to drink, I was a stranger and you welcomed me, I was naked and you gave me clothing, I was sick and you took care of me, I was in prison and you visited me.' Then the righteous will answer him, 'Lord, when was it that we saw you hungry and gave you food, or thirsty and gave you something to drink? And when was it that we saw you a stranger and welcomed you, or naked and gave you clothing? And when was it that we saw you sick or in prison and visited you?' And the king will answer them, 'Truly I tell you, just as you did it to one of the least of these who are members of my family, you did it to me.'"

- The Last Judgment, the *Dies Irae*, stirs my heart with fear. Yet in the end, Lord, your message is simple, your command easy. You are there beside me in the needy.

- I have only to reach them to reach you.

**Tuesday 12th February**        **Matthew 6:11**

Give us this day our daily bread.

- The Greek word translated as "daily" is *epiousios*. Until recently it was unknown, occurring in this sentence in the Gospel but nowhere else in ancient literature. Then on a fragment of papyrus they found the word on a woman's shopping list, indicating that she needed to get supplies of a certain food for the coming day.

- That is the deep meaning of this workaday word: Lord, give me what I need to get through the day, to manage my business, keep the children happy, and survive myself. Give me thy love and grace just for today.

**Wednesday 13th February**        **Jonah 3:1–5**

The word of the Lord came to Jonah a second time, saying, "Get up, go to Nineveh, that great city, and proclaim to it the message that I tell you." So Jonah set out and went to Nineveh, according to the word of the Lord. Now Nineveh was an exceedingly large city, a three days' walk across. Jonah began to go into the city, going a day's walk. And he cried out, "Forty days more, and Nineveh shall be overthrown!" And the people of Nineveh believed God; they proclaimed a fast, and everyone, great and small, put on sackcloth.

- Sin is a reality in the life of every one of us, but so is God's mercy and forgiveness. Sin is not a matter of committing any one of a list of forbidden acts, but a decision to turn away from God.

- If I am honest with myself, I know when I am doing this. Is there some area of my life where this is going on, where I am keeping God out, because doing the right thing might be inconvenient? The good news is: all I have to do is turn back.

### Thursday 14th February    Mathew 7:7–11

Jesus said to the crowds, "Ask, and it will be given you; search, and you will find; knock, and the door will be opened for you. For everyone who asks receives, and everyone who searches finds, and for everyone who knocks, the door will be opened. Is there anyone among you who, if your child asks for bread, will give a stone? Or if the child asks for a fish, will give a snake? If you then, who are evil, know how to give good gifts to your children, how much more will your Father in heaven give good things to those who ask him!"

- "Ask . . . search . . . knock." Three aspects of prayer, each one giving us confidence of gaining a hearing. Jesus' teaching is demanding, but our Father is willing to give us the capacity if we but ask.

• With the confidence of the child, we can demand, "Give us this day our daily bread." Each day, we are invited to ask, to demand.

**Friday 15th February      Matthew 5:20–26**

J esus said to his disciples, "For I tell you, unless your righteousness exceeds that of the scribes and Pharisees, you will never enter the kingdom of heaven. You have heard that it was said to those of ancient times, 'You shall not murder;' and 'whoever murders shall be liable to judgment.' But I say to you that if you are angry with a brother or sister, you will be liable to judgment; and if you insult a brother or sister, you will be liable to the council; and if you say, 'You fool,' you will be liable to the hell of fire. So when you are offering your gift at the altar, if you remember that your brother or sister has something against you, leave your gift there before the altar and go; first be reconciled to your brother or sister, and then come and offer your gift. Come to terms quickly with your accuser while you are on the way to court with him, or your accuser may hand you over to the judge, and the judge to the guard, and you will be thrown into prison. Truly I tell you, you will never get out until you have paid the last penny."

- Must I repress and deny all anger? You might as well deny feeling hot in the Sahara. The feeling is innocent; there are times when anger sweeps over me and has to be acknowledged. The evil arises when I act out my anger by bad-mouthing or injuring my neighbor, and when I give way to hatred.

- Lord, I come before your altar. Help me to work on the seeds of hatred in my heart. You tell me that there can be no true worship of God without justice.

## Saturday 16th February   Matthew 5:43–48

Jesus said to the disciples, "You have heard that it was said, 'You shall love your neighbor and hate your enemy.' But I say to you, love your enemies and pray for those who persecute you, so that you may be children of your Father in heaven; for he makes his sun rise on the evil and on the good, and sends rain on the righteous and on the unrighteous. For if you love those who love you, what reward do you have? Do not even the tax collectors do the same? And if you greet only your brothers and sisters, what more are you doing than others? Do not even the Gentiles do the same? Be perfect, therefore, as your heavenly Father is perfect."

- There is a footnote to the biblical story of the Egyptian army being drowned in the Red Sea, while the Jews escaped dry-footed. The rabbis imagined the angels starting a paean of praise to God, but the Lord interrupting them sadly: The work of my hands are sunk in the sea, and you would sing before me!

- When Jesus bids us be perfect like God, he means that we try to love as generously and universally as God, and to be good even to those who dislike us.

# february 17–23

Something to think and pray about each day this week:

## Learning What We Know

In prayer we are *reminded* rather than *changed*. Prayer helps us to realize what we already know. The Holy Spirit is not an alien invader, but the one who enables us to be ourselves. On Good Friday, Peter and the apostles had the same personalities as they would have on Pentecost, but they lacked the courage to be themselves, to speak out from their hearts about what they had heard from Jesus. The apostles at Pentecost did not get more lectures on Christianity. Instead they gained the confidence to use what they already knew. Paddy Kavanagh, the Irish poet, used to say that we only learn what we already know. We learn by reflecting on our experience.

## The Presence of God

I pause for a moment
aware that God is here.
I think of how everything around me
the air I breathe, my whole body,
is tingling with the presence of God.

## Freedom

I will ask God's help
to be free from my own preoccupations,
to be open to God in this time of prayer,
to come to love and serve him more.

## Consciousness

In God's loving presence
I unwind the past day
starting from now and looking back,

moment by moment, I gather
all the goodness and light, in gratitude.
I attend to all the shadows
and what they say to me
seeking healing, courage, and forgiveness.

## The Word

I take my time to read the word of God, slowly, a few times, allowing myself to dwell on anything that strikes me. (Please turn to your scripture on the following pages. Inspiration points are there should you need them. When you are ready, return here to continue.)

## Conversation

Sometimes I wonder what I might say
if I were to meet You in person, Lord.
I might say "Thank you, Lord"
for always being there for me.
I know with certainty
there were times when you carried me.

When through your strength
I got through the dark times in my life.

## Conclusion

Glory be to the Father, and to the Son, and
to the Holy Spirit, as it was in the beginning,
is now and ever shall be, world without end.
Amen.

## Sunday 17th February,
## Second Sunday of Lent          Genesis 12:1–4

Now the LORD said to Abram, "Go from your country and your kindred and your father's house to the land that I will show you. I will make of you a great nation, and I will bless you, and make your name great, so that you will be a blessing. I will bless those who bless you, and the one who curses you I will curse; and in you all the families of the earth shall be blessed." So Abram went, as the LORD had told him; and Lot went with him. Abram was seventy-five years old when he departed from Haran.

• God said to Abraham: "By you all the families of the earth shall bless themselves." Christians, Moslems, and Jews are all children of Abraham. The future of civilization may depend on relishing what we share with Islam rather than focusing on our differences.

- Can we become a blessing to all the families of the earth, by our reverence and love for the one, true, and compassionate God? I marvel at the fidelity to daily prayer, and at the reverence for God shown by devout Moslems.

- Religion at its best can only unite people.

**Monday 18th February**          Luke 6:36–38

"Be merciful, just as your Father is merciful. Do not judge, and you will not be judged; do not condemn, and you will not be condemned. Forgive, and you will be forgiven; give, and it will be given to you. A good measure, pressed down, shaken together, running over, will be put into your lap; for the measure you give will be the measure you get back."

- Can I remember times when I heard people gossip about me, with no understanding of why I behaved as I did? Can I remember times when I leapt to judge others without knowing the whys and wherefores? Remember the Sioux prayer: May I never judge another until I have walked in his moccasins. Good newspapers offer us information without judgments. Shoddy papers try to do our thinking for us, leap to take sides, and express their judgments in banner headlines.

- Lord, keep me from jumping to judgment. You alone know all that is my heart and in the hearts of those I am tempted to condemn.

**Tuesday 19th February        Isaiah 1:16–17**

Wash yourselves; make yourselves clean; remove the evil of your doings from before my eyes; cease to do evil, learn to do good; seek justice, rescue the oppressed, defend the orphan, plead for the widow.

- Lord, thank you for calling me to attention. There is no point in me following religious observances diligently if I continue to ignore suffering and injustice around me.
- Teach me to be just, so that I pray with a clean heart and give praise to your name.

## Wednesday 20th February

### Matthew 20:17–19

While Jesus was going up to Jerusalem, he took the twelve disciples aside by themselves, and said to them on the way, "See, we are going up to Jerusalem, and the Son of Man will be handed over to the chief priests and scribes, and they will condemn him to death; then they will hand him over to the Gentiles to be mocked and flogged and crucified; and on the third day he will be raised."

- There is a sense of doom and destiny in Jesus' words. Like Captain Oates going out into the

Antarctic night: "I am just going outside and may be some time." Or like Aslan, the heroic lion in Narnia, walking alone into the hands of the White Witch.

• The anticipation of personal catastrophe chills the heart. When Jesus foretells the passion, he mentions not just the handover, but the flogging and mocking. It is hard to imagine the terror that must have shadowed his heart in those last weeks.

**Thursday 21st February    Jeremiah 17:5–8**

Thus says the Lord: Cursed are those who trust in mere mortals and make mere flesh their strength, whose hearts turn away from the Lord. They shall be like a shrub in the desert, and shall not see when relief comes. They shall live in the parched places of the wilderness, in an uninhabited salt land. Blessed are those who trust in the Lord, whose trust is the

Lord. They shall be like a tree planted by water, sending out its roots by the stream. It shall not fear when heat comes, and its leaves shall stay green; in the year of drought it is not anxious, and it does not cease to bear fruit.

- Lord, I know that wilderness feeling, when I am blown about like a paper bag in the wind, up and down, at the mercy of each day's events. I remember too the times when I felt rooted in you, trusting you, sensing the water of your nourishment even in bad times.

- Let me be that tree planted by water, sending out its roots to the stream of your goodness.

## Friday 22nd February,
## The See of St. Peter          Matthew 16:13–19

Now when Jesus came into the district of Caesarea Philippi, he asked his disciples, "Who do people say that the Son of Man is?"

And they said, "Some say John the Baptist, but others Elijah, and still others Jeremiah or one of the prophets." He said to them, "But who do you say that I am?" Simon Peter answered, "You are the Messiah, the Son of the living God." And Jesus answered him, "Blessed are you, Simon son of Jonah! For flesh and blood has not revealed this to you, but my Father in heaven. And I tell you, you are Peter, and on this rock I will build my church, and the gates of Hades will not prevail against it. I will give you the keys of the kingdom of heaven, and whatever you bind on earth will be bound in heaven, and whatever you loose on earth will be loosed in heaven."

- When I see the failings of the church, I wonder about its foundation on the rock. Then I think: the gates of hell—sometimes in the shape of inner corruption—have not prevailed. The people of God are still vigorous, and growing, and holy in countless hidden ways, still sustained by the vision of God made visible in Jesus.

- I can still echo Peter: You are the son of the living God.

## Saturday 23rd February    Luke 15:20–24

While the son was still far off, his father saw him and was filled with compassion; he ran and put his arms around him and kissed him. Then the son said to him, "Father, I have sinned against heaven and before you; I am no longer worthy to be called your son." But the father said to his slaves, "Quickly, bring out a robe—the best one—and put it on him; put a ring on his finger and sandals on his feet. And get the fatted calf and kill it, and let us eat and celebrate; for this son of mine was dead and is alive again; he was lost and is found!" And they began to celebrate.

- Jesus, this parable of the Prodigal Son was the closest you came to describing your heavenly Father: compassionate, generous, tender, watching out for me, not so much forgiving my sins as not noticing them—they are washed out of sight and mind by the Niagara of his love.

# february 24–march 1

Something to think and pray about each day this week:

## Sharing My Cross

You tell me to "carry my cross," Lord. You are not telling me to go out looking for the cross, in practices or penances, but rather to find it under my nose. Every encounter that costs me, that rubs off my ego, is part of your plan for me. I start with my own body and heart. The aches and limitations of my limbs, my awkwardness and shyness, are part of my cross. I often wish I was different, but this is me, and I will learn to love me as you do. When I can't think of anything to say in company, or when I think of the wrong things, I'm carrying my cross.

What consoles me is that you like my company. You can put up with my silences. You accept the grumpy mutterings that at times are the closest I come to conversation. I don't always feel good about myself. There are moments when, like Groucho Marx, I would not want to belong to any club that was ready to accept me as a member. You not merely accept me, but make me feel I belong, a first-born child in whom you delight.

## The Presence of God

I pause for a moment
and think of the love and the grace
that God showers on me,
creating me in his image and likeness,
making me his temple.

## Freedom

Everything has the potential
to draw forth from me

a fuller love and life.
Yet my desires are often fixed,
caught, on illusions of fulfillment.
I ask that God, through my freedom,
may orchestrate my desires
in a vibrant loving melody rich in harmony.

## Consciousness

In the presence of my loving Creator,
I look honestly at my feelings
over the last day,
the highs, the lows, and the level ground.
Can I see where the Lord has been present?

## The Word

God speaks to each one of us individually.
I need to listen to what he is saying to me.
(Please turn to your scripture on the following
pages. Inspiration points are there should you
need them. When you are ready, return here
to continue.)

## Conversation

What feelings are rising in me
as I pray and reflect on God's word?
I imagine Jesus himself sitting beside me,
and open my heart to him.

## Conclusion

Glory be to the Father, and to the Son, and
to the Holy Spirit, as it was in the beginning,
is now and ever shall be, world without end.
Amen.

## Sunday 24th February,
## Third Sunday of Lent          John 4:5–12

So he came to a Samaritan city called Sychar, near the plot of ground that Jacob had given to his son Joseph. Jacob's well was there, and Jesus, tired out by his journey, was sitting by the well. It was about noon. A Samaritan woman came to draw water, and Jesus said to her, "Give me a drink." (His disciples had gone to the city to buy food.) The Samaritan woman said to him, "How is it that you, a Jew, ask a drink of me, a woman of Samaria?" (Jews do not share things in common with Samaritans.) Jesus answered her, "If you knew the gift of God, and who it is that is saying to you, 'Give me a drink,' you would have asked him, and he would have given you living water." The woman said to him, "Sir, you have no bucket, and the well is deep. Where do you get that living water? Are you greater than our ancestor Jacob, who gave us the well, and with his sons and his flocks drank from it?"

- When Jesus crosses these religious and social barriers, speaking to this woman who is also a Samaritan, she does not retreat but responds— first in astonishment and then with curiosity.

- In her astonishment she is open to new possibilities; in her curiosity she is willing to explore what they might be.

- How am I responding to Jesus' message? Am I still curious? Do I want to know more, or have I "switched off"?

## Monday 25th February          Luke 4:24–30

And he said, "Truly I tell you, no prophet is accepted in the prophet's hometown. But the truth is, there were many widows in Israel in the time of Elijah, when the heaven was shut up three years and six months, and there was a severe famine over all the land; yet Elijah was sent to none of them except to a widow at Zarephath in Sidon. There were also many lepers in Israel in the time of the prophet Elisha, and none of them was cleansed except Naaman the Syrian." When they heard this, all in the synagogue were filled with rage. They got up, drove him out of the town, and led him to the brow of the hill on which their town was built, so that they might hurl him off the cliff. But he passed through the midst of them and went on his way.

- "When they heard this, all in the synagogue were filled with rage." When we have fixed views, when our deepest expectations are confronted and overturned, then our reactions may lead us even to violence—such is the pain and offence we can feel.

- How do I categorize people, and on what basis: on appearance? family? race? nationality? What did Jesus do? Can I imitate him?

## Tuesday 26th February        Daniel 3:38–41

We now have no leader, no prophet, no Prince, no burnt offering, no sacrifice, no oblation, no incense, no place where we can make offerings to you and win your favor. But may the contrite soul, the humbled spirit, be as acceptable to you as burnt offerings of rams and bullocks, as thousands of fat lambs: such let our sacrifice be to you today, and may it please you that we follow you wholeheartedly, since those who trust in you will not be shamed. And now we put our whole heart into following you, into fearing you and seeking your face once more.

- Azariah makes this prayer when all seems lost, when he and his companions are facing death for refusing to worship false gods.

- What is my prayer like when I hit rock bottom? When the news is sickening, and my life is in shreds, can I still put my heart into seeking God's face?

- But God, who knows me intimately, with all my strengths and weaknesses, is still more interested in me than in all the riches and lavish offerings other people might have to make.

## Wednesday 27th February

### Deuteronomy 4:5–9

See, just as the Lord my God has charged me, I now teach you statutes and ordinances for you to observe in the land that you are about to enter and occupy. You must observe them diligently, for this will show your wisdom and discernment to the peoples, who, when they hear all these statutes, will say, "Surely this great nation is a wise and discerning people!" For what other great nation has a god so near to it as the Lord our God is whenever we call? And what other great nation has statutes and ordinances as just as this entire law that I am setting before you today? But take care and watch yourselves closely, so as neither to forget the things that your eyes have seen nor to let them slip from your mind all the days of your life; make them known to your children and your children's children.

- Lord, as the world around me changes fast, how can I find the language to pass on your word to the next generation? Teach me to make your wisdom the code of my heart, and then I shall be able to speak of it from my heart.

**Thursday 28th February**      **Jeremiah 7:23**

But this command I gave them, "Obey my voice, and I will be your God, and you shall be my people; and walk only in the way that I command you, so that it may be well with you."

- What way do I walk in, Lord? Sometimes it is the highway of immediate pleasure, sometimes the by-way of devious plotting, sometimes the shadowy lane of resentment or depression. I want to walk in the path of faithful love.
- Keep my feet from straying.

**Friday 29th February     Hosea 14:2, 4–7**

Take words with you and return to the Lord; say to him, "Take away all guilt; accept that which is good, and we will offer the fruit of our lips. . . . I will heal their disloyalty; I will love them freely, for my anger has turned from them. I will be like the dew to Israel; he shall blossom like the lily, he shall strike root like the forests of Lebanon. His shoots shall spread out; his beauty shall be like the olive tree, and his fragrance like that of Lebanon. They shall again live beneath my shadow, they shall flourish as a garden; they shall blossom like the vine, their fragrance shall be like the wine of Lebanon.

- Lord, what lovely images these words of Hosea offer! Like the dew you make me blossom, spread my fragrance like the bouquet of good wine, flourish like a garden, my roots deep and firm.

- Wash away my guilt, Lord. That distorts me more than anything. Your love washes away my guilt, leaves me clean and smelling sweet.

## Saturday 1st March      Luke 18:9–14

He also told this parable to some who trusted in themselves that they were righteous and regarded others with contempt: "Two men went up to the Temple to pray, one a Pharisee and the other a tax collector. The Pharisee, standing by himself, was praying thus, 'God, I thank you that I am not like other people: thieves, rogues, adulterers, or even like this tax collector. I fast twice a week; I give a tenth of all my income.' But the tax collector, standing far off, would not even look up to heaven, but was beating his breast and saying, 'God, be merciful to me, a sinner!' I tell you, this man went down to his home justified rather than the other; for all who exalt themselves will be humbled, but all who humble themselves will be exalted."

- The contrast between Pharisee and tax collector has entered so deeply into our culture; Pharisee, a term of honor in Jesus' society, is not something we want to be called. To place it in our culture, read convicted rapist, pedophile, tyrant; any hate-figure of the popular press. We are sometimes persuaded to despise them as the Pharisee despised the humble tax collector. It is not for us to look down on anyone.

- How does the story hit me? I fear being an object of people's contempt. But Lord, if they knew me as you do, they might be right to feel contempt. I have no right to look down on those whose sins are paraded in the media. Be merciful to me.

# march 2–8

Something to think and pray about each day this week:

## The Joy of Freedom

The fourth Sunday of Lent was once called *Laetare* Sunday, an invitation to gaiety in a somber season. Some churches treasured rose-colored vestments which they showed off, in place of the purple, on this Sunday and on the third of Advent. It made sense. The sort of self-control that we aim at in Lent can lift our hearts and give us a sense of freedom. We feel at peace because we are in charge of our appetites, not vice versa. People who visit Carmelites, or others of austere life, are astonished to find that there is more laughter in the convent than outside. Nietzsche and Thomas

Aquinas agree on one thing. The gloomy pagan admitted: "The mother of dissipation is not joy but joylessness." The saintly Dominican put it more positively: "A joyful heart is a sign of temperance." We still have half of Lent in which to claw back some of our inner freedom and joy.

## The Presence of God

I reflect for a moment
on God's presence around me and in me.
Creator of the universe,
the sun and the moon, the earth,
every molecule, every atom,
everything that is:
God is in every beat of my heart.
God is with me, now.

## Freedom

"A thick and shapeless tree-trunk would never believe that it could become

a statue, admired as a miracle of sculpture,
and would never submit itself
to the chisel of the sculptor, who sees by her
genius what she can make of it" (St. Ignatius).
I ask for the grace to let myself be shaped
by my loving Creator.

## Consciousness

Knowing that God loves me unconditionally,
I look honestly over the last day,
its events and my feelings.
Do I have something to be grateful for?
Then I give thanks.
Is there something I am sorry for?
Then I ask forgiveness.

## The Word

I read the word of God slowly, a few times
over, and I listen to what God is saying to me.
(Please turn to your scripture on the following
pages. Inspiration points are there should you

need them. When you are ready, return here
to continue.)

## Conversation

What is stirring in me as I pray?
Am I consoled, troubled, left cold?
I imagine Jesus sitting beside me,
and share my feelings with him.

## Conclusion

Glory be to the Father, and to the Son, and to
the Holy Spirit, as it was in the beginning, is
now and ever shall be, world without end.
Amen.

**Sunday 2nd March,**
**Fourth Sunday of Lent**     **John 9:1–3, 6–7**

As Jesus walked along, he saw a man blind from birth. His disciples asked him, "Rabbi, who sinned, this man or his parents, that he was born blind?" Jesus answered, "Neither this man nor his parents sinned; he was born blind so that God's works might be revealed in him. . . ." When he had said this, he spat on the ground and made mud with the saliva and spread the mud on the man's eyes, saying to him, "Go, wash in the pool of Siloam" (which means Sent). Then he went and washed and came back able to see.

- In many parts of the ancient world, the spittle of good people was believed to be curative. In using his spittle Jesus was doing what the patient believed a doctor would do; like a good healer he built on the expectation of the sick person.

- Beyond that, Jesus was revealing the power of God. Sickness and misfortune can be a chance to show the glory of God working in our own lives.
- Lord, keep me open to you when tragedy really strikes. Let me feel your hand there.

**Monday 3rd March**　　　**John 4:46b–54**

Now there was a royal official whose son lay ill in Capernaum. When he heard that Jesus had come from Judea to Galilee, he went and begged him to come down and heal his son, for he was at the point of death. Then Jesus said to him, "Unless you see signs and wonders you will not believe." The official said to him, "Sir, come down before my little boy dies." Jesus said to him, "Go; your son will live." The man believed the word that Jesus spoke to him and started on his way. As he was going down, his slaves met him and told him that his child was alive. So he asked them the hour when he began to recover, and they said to him, "Yesterday at one in the afternoon the fever left him." The father realized that this was the hour when Jesus had said to him, "Your son will live." So he himself believed, along with his whole household. Now this was the second sign that Jesus did after coming from Judea to Galilee.

- "Your son will live," said Jesus who was coming ever closer to his own death, his "hour"; this sign points toward the new life, the new creation that is to come.

- Like the boy's father, can I believe, can I put my trust in God?

**Tuesday 4th March**          **John 5:1–8**

After this there was a festival of the Jews, and Jesus went up to Jerusalem. Now in Jerusalem by the Sheep Gate there is a pool, called in Hebrew Beth-zatha, which has five porticoes. In these lay many invalids—blind, lame, and paralyzed. One man was there who had been ill for thirty-eight years. When Jesus saw him lying there and knew that he had been there a long time, he said to him, "Do you want to be made well?" The sick man answered him, "Sir, I have no one to put me into the pool when the water is stirred up; and while I am making my way, someone else steps down ahead of me." Jesus said to him, "Stand up, take your mat and walk."

•   What a strange question Jesus asked: Do you want to be made well? Yet for those who have been sick for years, a cure is a jolting change in their lives, from dependence and care to managing for themselves.

- Do I really want to be healed of all the physical and spiritual ailments I complain of? Am I ready for a change in my life?

**Wednesday 5th March      Isaiah 49.14–16**

Zion said, "The Lord has forsaken me, my Lord has forgotten me." Can a woman forget her nursing child, or show no compassion for the child of her womb? Even these may forget, yet I will not forget you. See, I have inscribed you on the palms of my hands; your walls are continually before me.

- In this passage the Bible moves from the image of a heavenly father to the image of a heavenly mother. No human passion is as strong as that of a mother for her child. The baby is part of her, unforgettable.

- The grief of the mother whose baby has died is something that men can hardly imagine. That visceral passion is ascribed here to God, who is beyond gender, but the source of all love.

**Thursday 6th March          Psalm 106:19–24**

They made a calf at Horeb and worshiped a cast image. They exchanged the glory of God for the image of an ox that eats grass. They forgot God, their Savior, who had done great things in Egypt, wondrous works in the land of Ham, and awesome deeds by the Red Sea. Therefore he said he would destroy them—had not Moses, his chosen one, stood in the breach before him, to turn away his wrath from destroying them. Then they despised the pleasant land, having no faith in his promise.

- I'd better not judge the Chosen People too harshly. As I wander through my particular desert, what golden calves have caught my eye? No point dwelling too long on golden calves!

- "They forgot the God who was their Savior." It is all about remembering, constantly.

**Friday 7th March          Wisdom 2:1, 12–15**

For the godless reasoned unsoundly, saying to themselves, "Short and sorrowful is our life, and there is no remedy when a life comes to its end, and no one has been known to return from Hades. Let us lie in wait for the righteous man, because he is inconvenient to us and opposes our actions; he reproaches us for sins against the law, and accuses us of sins against our training. He professes to have knowledge of God, and calls himself a child of the Lord. He became to us a reproof of our thoughts; the very sight of him is a burden to us, because his manner of life is unlike that of others, and his ways are strange."

- Who do I identify with, Lord? I can grasp what the godless are feeling because I have sometimes felt the same niggling resentment when my mediocrity is shown up by the integrity of some good person.

- Have I the courage to stand up for goodness, and to take the criticism and hostility that will provoke?

## Saturday 8th March                    John 7:40–47

When they heard these words, some in the crowd said, "This is really the prophet." Others said, "This is the Messiah." But some asked, "Surely the Messiah does not come from Galilee, does he? Has not the scripture said that the Messiah is descended from David and comes from Bethlehem, the village where David lived?" So there was a division in the crowd because of him. Some of them wanted to arrest him, but no one laid hands on him.

Then the Temple police went back to the chief priests and Pharisees, who asked them, "Why did you not arrest him?" The police answered, "Never has anyone spoken like this!" Then the Pharisees replied, "Surely you have not been deceived too, have you?"

- Here are two ways of approaching Jesus: some hear him, see how he lives, and love and enjoy him. Others go back to their books and argue about his pedigree.

- Lord, save me from losing you in the babble of books and arguments. May I meet and know and enjoy you.

# march 9–15

Something to think and pray about each day this week:

## Freedom and Forgiveness

This fifth Sunday of Lent was once called Passion Sunday, and statues and ornaments in churches were covered in purple until Easter. Although that title has now been moved to next Sunday, we can still consider these two weeks Passiontide. They are spent in the shadow of Calvary. Jesus' enemies are smelling victory. The just and innocent man is to be framed by false allegations and put to death. We are struggling with the ancient problem of evil: Why do the wicked prosper? But in the passion of Jesus the wicked do not defeat goodness.

They do not drive him to despair or bitterness. His heart remains free and forgiving. We have known such moments in our own lives. Have our hearts turned to blame and bitterness, or are they free?

## The Presence of God

In the silence of my innermost being,
in the fragments of my yearned-for wholeness,
can I hear the whispers of God's presence?
Can I remember when I felt God's nearness?
When we walked together
and I let myself be embraced by God's love.

## Freedom

"There are very few people who realize what God would make of them if they abandoned themselves into his hands, and let themselves be formed by his grace" (St. Ignatius).
I ask for the grace
to trust myself totally to God's love.

## Consciousness

I exist in a web of relationships,
links to nature, people, God.
I trace out these links, giving thanks
for the love that flows through them.
If I feel regret, anger, disappointment,
I pray for the gift of acceptance and forgiveness.

## The Word

The word of God comes down to us through
the scriptures. May the Holy Spirit enlighten
my mind and my heart to respond to the gospel teachings. (Please turn to your scripture
on the following pages. Inspiration points are
there should you need them. When you are
ready, return here to continue.)

## Conversation

Do I notice myself reacting
as I pray with the word of God?
Do I feel challenged, comforted, angry?

I imagine Jesus sitting beside me,
I speak out my feelings,
as one trusted friend to another.

## Conclusion

Glory be to the Father, and to the Son, and
to the Holy Spirit, as it was in the beginning,
is now and ever shall be, world without end.
Amen.

## Sunday 9th March,
## Fifth Sunday of Lent          John 11:32–37

When Mary came where Jesus was and saw him, she knelt at his feet and said to him, "Lord, if you had been here, my brother would not have died." When Jesus saw her weeping, and the Jews who came with her also weeping, he was greatly disturbed in spirit and deeply moved. He said, "Where have you laid him?" They said to him, "Lord, come and see." Jesus began to weep. So the Jews said, "See how he loved him!" But some of them said, "Could not he who opened the eyes of the blind man have kept this man from dying?"

- "Jesus wept." Lord, you are not a cold icon. You are as vulnerable as we are to sadness, loss, and grief. Remember me by name. Keep me a place in your heart as you had a place for Lazarus.

## Monday 10th March

### Daniel 13:55–56, 60–62

Daniel said, "Indeed! Your lie recoils on your own head: the angel of God has already received from him your sentence and will cut you in half." He dismissed the man, ordered the other to be brought and said to him, "Son of Canaan, not of Judah, beauty has seduced you, lust has led your heart astray!" Then the whole assembly shouted, blessing God, the Savior of those who trust in him. And they turned on the two elders whom Daniel had convicted of false evidence out of their own mouths. As the Law of Moses prescribes, they were given the same punishment as they had schemed to inflict on their neighbor. They were put to death. And thus, that day, an innocent life was saved.

• "Beauty has deceived you and lust has perverted your heart." Plenty of others—more men than women—have followed those old men in being led by lust into personal disaster. Out-of-control hormones can trigger what looks from the outside like self-destructive madness.

- These are not happy characters. Dissipation and addiction are forms of imprisonment in which the chains are inside us, not outside; so the pain is greater.

- Thomas Aquinas said: "A joyful heart is a sure sign of temperance and self-control." Do I show that sign?

## Tuesday 11th March      Numbers 21:4–9

From Mount Hor they set out by the way to the Red Sea, to go around the land of Edom; but the people became impatient on the way. The people spoke against God and against Moses, "Why have you brought us up out of Egypt to die in the wilderness? For there is no food and no water, and we detest this miserable food." Then the LORD sent poisonous serpents among the people, and they bit the people, so that many Israelites died. The people came to Moses and said, "We have sinned by speaking against the LORD and against you; pray to the LORD to take away the serpents from us." So Moses prayed for the people. And the LORD said to Moses, "Make a poisonous serpent, and set it on a pole; and everyone who is bitten shall look at it and live." So Moses made a serpent of bronze, and put it upon a pole; and whenever a serpent bit someone, that person would look at the serpent of bronze and live.

- That image of a coiled serpent still adorns clinics to symbolize the healing work of doctors. It prefigures the image of Jesus raised up on the cross, an image that can heal bitterness and self-pity when we are in the wilderness.

- How am I affected by the challenge to be a healer?

## Wednesday 12th March      John 8:31–32

Then Jesus said to the Jews who had believed in him, "If you continue in my word, you are truly my disciples; and you will know the truth, and the truth will make you free."

- That is a grand, bold phrase: "The truth will make you free." It is used in all sorts of modern rhetoric, but when it comes to the crunch, it can terrify me.

- But can I handle the truth: of my own addictions? of the unfaithfulness of somebody close to me? of the signs in my body of approaching death?

- Yet when I acknowledge such truths, they can liberate me.

**Thursday 13th March**     **Genesis 17:3–8**

Then Abram fell on his face; and God said to him, "As for me, this is my covenant with you: You shall be the ancestor of a multitude of nations. No longer shall your name be Abram, but your name shall be Abraham; for I have made you the ancestor of a multitude of nations. I will make you exceedingly fruitful; and I will make nations of you, and kings shall come from you. I will establish my covenant between me and you, and your offspring after you throughout their generations, for an everlasting covenant, to be God to you and to your offspring after you. And I will give to you, and to your offspring after you, the land where you are now an alien, all the land of Canaan, for a perpetual holding; and I will be their God."

• Father Abraham, the common spiritual ancestor for Christians, Jews, and Moslems, is more important than ever today. If we children of Abraham, in these three great religions, could rediscover and cherish all that we have in common, the world would be a safer place.

- What can I do to move this process along?

## Friday 14th March                 Psalm 18:1–3

I love you, O LORD, my strength. The LORD is my rock, my fortress, and my deliverer, my God, my rock in whom I take refuge, my shield, and the horn of my salvation, my stronghold. I call upon the LORD, who is worthy to be praised, so I shall be saved from my enemies.

- Thank you, Lord, for the simple psalms. They remain with me when my head has abandoned faith, and all that is left is a sense of needing God desperately. Then I can cry out, "I love you, O Lord, my strength."

**Saturday 15th March**  **John 11:47–52**

So the chief priests and the Pharisees called a meeting of the council, and said, "What are we to do? This man is performing many signs. If we let him go on like this, everyone will believe in him, and the Romans will come and destroy both our holy place and our nation." But one of them, Caiaphas, who was high priest that year, said to them, "You know nothing at all! You do not understand that it is better for you to have one man die for the people than to have the whole nation destroyed." He did not say this on his own, but being high priest that year he prophesied that Jesus was about to die for the nation, and not for the nation only, but to gather into one the dispersed children of God.

- Caiaphas was a Sadducee; ruthless, political, determined to buttress the status quo and the privileges of his class. He uses the argument of the powerful in every age: we must eliminate the awkward troublemaker in the name of the common good—namely, the comfort of Sadducees.

- This man spoke more wisely than he knew. One man, Jesus, was to die for the people, and for me.

Something to think and pray about each day this week:

## The Model of Prayer

Jesus moves toward his fate as the Jews stumbled into the gas chambers of Auschwitz, calling on God but hearing no answer. The more we know of suffering, the harder it is to live fully in this week of the passion. Yet Jesus in Gethsemani is the model of prayer. He shows no self-pity. The chalice of rejection and torture seems humanly unbearable and he asks God to let it pass from him. Like us, he has to interpret not just God's dialogues with him, but also God's silence. Jesus redeems us not by his miracles and preaching, but by his suffering. When he accepts the chalice, he rises strong to meet his executioners. It is our human duty to fight suffering, but there are times when like Jesus we are reduced to passivity and passion.

## The Presence of God

God is with me, but more,
God is within me, giving me existence.
Let me dwell for a moment
on God's life-giving presence
in my body, my mind, my heart
and in the whole of my life.

## Freedom

Many countries are, at this moment,
suffering the agonies of war.
I bow my head in thanksgiving for my freedom.
I pray for all prisoners and captives.

## Consciousness

I remind myself that I am in the presence of
the Lord.
I will take refuge in his loving heart.
He is my strength in times of weakness.
He is my comforter in times of sorrow.

## The Word

I take my time to read the word of God, slowly, a few times, allowing myself to dwell on
anything that strikes me. (Please turn to your
scripture on the following pages. Inspiration
points are there should you need them. When
you are ready, return here to continue.)

## Conversation

Remembering that I am
still in God's presence,
I imagine Jesus himself sitting beside me,
and say whatever is on my mind,

whatever is in my heart,
speaking as one friend to another.

## Conclusion

Glory be to the Father, and to the Son, and
to the Holy Spirit, as it was in the beginning,
is now and ever shall be, world without end.
Amen.

## Sunday 16th March, Palm Sunday
## of the Lord's Passion          Matthew 21:1–11

When they had come near Jerusalem and had reached Bethpage, at the Mount of Olives, Jesus sent two disciples, saying to them, "Go into the village ahead of you, and immediately you will find a donkey tied, and a colt with her; untie them and bring them to me. If anyone says anything to you, just say this, 'The Lord needs them.' And he will send them immediately." This took place to fulfill what had been spoken through the prophet, saying, "Tell the daughter of Zion, Look, your king is coming to you, humble, and mounted on a donkey, and on a colt, the foal of a donkey." The disciples went and did as Jesus had directed them; they brought the donkey and the colt, and put their cloaks on them, and he sat on them. A very large crowd spread their cloaks on the road, and others cut branches from the trees and spread them on the road. The crowds that went ahead of him and that followed were shouting, "Hosanna to the Son of David! Blessed is the one who comes in the name of the Lord! Hosanna in the highest heaven!" When he entered Jerusalem, the whole city was in turmoil, asking, "Who is this?" The crowds were saying, "This is the prophet Jesus from Nazareth in Galilee."

- "Who is this?" As we recall this joyous celebration of the arrival of the prophet, Jesus of Nazareth, we are also aware of what lies ahead, as Jesus was.

- At the start of this momentous week, let me sit and ponder this familiar story. Can I read it afresh, as though for the first time?

## Monday 17th March         John 12:1–8

Six days before the Passover Jesus came to Bethany, the home of Lazarus, whom he had raised from the dead. There they gave a dinner for him. Martha served, and Lazarus was one of those at the table with him. Mary took a pound of costly perfume made of pure nard, anointed Jesus' feet, and wiped them with her hair. The house was filled with the fragrance of the perfume. But Judas Iscariot, one of his disciples (the one who was about to betray him), said, "Why was this perfume not sold for three hundred denarii and the money given to the poor?" (He said this not because he cared about the poor, but because he was a thief; he kept the common purse and used to steal what was put into it.) Jesus said, "Leave her alone. She bought it so that she might keep it for the day of my burial. You always have the poor with you, but you do not always have me."

- Can I sit with this scene for a while? A poignant reunion and family meal become heavy with drama, and with the portents of Jesus' death and resurrection. Meanwhile, Judas' focus is elsewhere.

• Teach me, Lord, to keep my eyes fixed on you.

## Tuesday 18th March
### John 13:21–27, 31–33, 36–38

After saying this Jesus was troubled in spirit, and declared, "Very truly, I tell you, one of you will betray me." The disciples looked at one another, uncertain of whom he was speaking. One of his disciples—the one whom Jesus loved—was reclining next to him; Simon Peter therefore motioned to him to ask Jesus of whom he was speaking. So while reclining next to Jesus, he asked him, "Lord, who is it?" Jesus answered, "It is the one to whom I give this piece of bread when I have dipped it in the dish." So when he had dipped the piece of bread, he gave it to Judas son of Simon Iscariot.

After he received the piece of bread, Satan entered into him. Jesus said to him, "Do quickly what you are going to do". . . . When Judas had gone out, Jesus said, "Now the Son of Man has been glorified, and God has been glorified in him. If God has been glorified in him, God will also glorify him in himself and will glorify him at once. Little children, I am with you only a little longer. You will look for me; and as I said to the Jews so now I say to you, 'Where I am going, you cannot come.' . . . Simon Peter said to him, "Lord, where are you going?" Jesus answered, "Where I am going, you cannot follow me now; but you will follow afterward." Peter said to him, "Lord, why can I not follow you now? I will lay down my life for you." Jesus answered, "Will you lay down your life for me? Very truly, I tell you, before the cock crows, you will have denied me three times."

- The gospel does not spare Simon Peter. We hear him protesting undying faithfulness, and before the night is out he acts the traitor. But it is unlike the treachery of Judas, who has plotted his betrayal and haggled over the price.

- Peter's denial of Jesus comes from the weakness of human respect, being shamed by a servant in Caiaphas's house.

- St. Philip Neri used to pray: "Lord, beware of this Philip or he will betray you! Lay your hand upon my head, for without you there is not a sin I may not commit this day."

## Wednesday 19th March  Isaiah 50:4–9

The Lord God has given me the tongue of a teacher, that I may know how to sustain the weary with a word. Morning by morning he wakens—wakens my ear to listen as those who are taught. The Lord God has opened my ear, and I was not rebellious, I did not turn backward. I gave my back to those who struck me, and my cheeks to those who pulled out the beard; I did not hide my face from insult and spitting. The Lord God helps me; therefore I have not been disgraced; therefore I have set my face like flint, and I know that I shall not be put to shame; he who vindicates me is near. Who will contend with me? Let us stand up together. Who are my adversaries? Let them confront me. It is the Lord God who helps me; who will declare me guilty? All of them will wear out like a garment; the moth will eat them up.

- Let us take our time to contemplate these wonderful words of the prophet Isaiah.

- This Suffering Servant is one who cares, a pupil, a listener, a person who asserts what is right, and one who persists to the end. Above all, this servant accepts all that comes from the Lord God.

### Thursday 20th March,
### Holy Thursday                    John 13:12–16

After Jesus had washed their feet, had put on his robe, and had returned to the table, he said to them, "Do you know what I have done to you? You call me Teacher and Lord—and you are right, for that is what I am. So if I, your Lord and Teacher, have washed your feet, you also ought to wash one another's feet. For I have set you an example, that you also should do as I have done to you. Very truly, I tell you, servants are not greater than their master, nor are messengers greater than the one who sent them."

- Where the other three gospels describe the Eucharist, John substitutes the washing of the feet. Why? From the beginning Christians have argued about the Eucharist; but works of service put us all on a level with Jesus, beyond argument.

- What used to be called menial work is no longer the job of slaves but the most secure way to God, Jesus has turned it from slave-work into an expression of love.

- Jesus kneeling with a towel round his waist is pointing to that aspect of Christianity in which there is no hierarchy, and the only rule is to meet the needs of others.

## Friday 21st March,
## Good Friday                    John 19:25–30

Meanwhile, standing near the cross of Jesus were his mother, and his mother's sister, Mary the wife of Clopas, and Mary Magdalene. When Jesus saw his mother and the disciple whom he loved standing beside her, he said to his mother, "Woman, here is your son." Then he said to the disciple, "Here is your mother." And from that hour the disciple took her into his own home. After this, when Jesus knew that all was now finished, he said (in order to fulfill the scripture), "I am thirsty." A jar full of sour wine was standing there. So they put a sponge full of the wine on a branch of hyssop and held it to his mouth. When Jesus had received the wine, he said, "It is finished." Then he bowed his head and gave up his spirit.

- Now we are at the heart of Jesus' mission: to suffer appallingly and to die without faltering in his love for us. This is where the gospel begins and ends.

- Love demands that we trust in a goodness and a life beyond our own. Lord, it is hard to contemplate. I pull away from the pain and injustice of this cross. God's love draws me back.

## Saturday 22nd March,
## Holy Saturday                    John 19:38–42

After these things, Joseph of Arimathea, who was a disciple of Jesus, though a secret one because of his fear of the Jews, asked Pilate to let him take away the body of Jesus. Pilate gave him permission; so he came and removed his body. Nicodemus, who had at first come to Jesus by night, also came, bringing a mixture of myrrh and aloes, weighing about a hundred pounds. They took the body of Jesus and wrapped it with the spices in linen cloths, according to the burial custom of the Jews. Now there was a garden in the place where he was crucified, and in the garden there was a new tomb in which no one had ever been laid. And so, because it was the Jewish day of preparation, and the tomb was nearby, they laid Jesus there.

- Joseph of Arimathea and Nicodemus were like many of us, secret admirers of Jesus, but afraid to raise their voice. They were members of the Sanhedrin which had framed the charge against Jesus. Out of fear they had stayed silent in that assembly, and now they were trying to make amends. A word in support of the living Jesus would have meant more than a new tomb, a load of spices and a shroud.

- Lord, may I not wait for a funeral to show my friends how I love and admire them.

# March 23

Something to think and pray about today:

## At the Center of Our Faith

This is a feast for our bodies, these marvelous shapely organisms that we have lived with for years, and are as central to us as our minds or memories. We shape our bodies, especially our faces, as the years pass. As the proverb says, the face we have at forty is the face that we deserve. But we feel the body's frailty in every scratch and hiccup, in every backache and sleepless night.

The apostles and the holy women did not see a ghost of Jesus. They saw him in the flesh, but in different flesh, as the oak tree is different from the acorn from which it grew. We touch on the mystery of a body, not just Jesus' body but our own. It will express us at our best, will not blunt our spirit with weariness and rebellion, but express it with ease and joy. This is a mystery beyond our imagination, but it is the center of our faith. As we grow older, nothing in our faith makes more sense than the passion and resurrection, the certainty that our body, like Jesus' body, must suffer and die, and the certainty that we, in our bodies, have a life beyond death.

## The Presence of God

To be present is to arrive as one is
and open up to the other.
At this instant, as I arrive here,
God is present waiting for me.
God always arrives before me,

desiring to connect with me
even more than my most intimate friend.
I take a moment and greet my loving God.

## Freedom

"In these days, God taught me as a school-
teacher teaches a pupil" (St. Ignatius).
I remind myself that there are things
God has yet to teach me,
and ask for the grace to hear them
and let them change me.

## Consciousness

How am I really feeling?
Light-hearted? Heavy-hearted?
I may be very much at peace,
happy to be here.
Equally, I may be frustrated,
worried or angry.

I acknowledge how I really am.
It is the real me that the Lord loves.

## The Word

God speaks to each one of us individually.
I need to listen to what he is saying to me.
(Please turn to your scripture on the following
pages. Inspiration points are there should you
need them. When you are ready, return here
to continue.)

## Conversation

How has God's word moved me?
Has it left me cold? Has it consoled me
or moved me to act in a new way?
I imagine Jesus sitting beside me,
I turn and share my feelings with him.

## Conclusion

Glory be to the Father, and to the Son, and to the Holy Spirit, as it was in the beginning, is now and ever shall be, world without end. Amen.

**Sunday 23rd March,**

**Easter Sunday**            John 20:1–9

Early on the first day of the week, while it was still dark, Mary Magdalene came to the tomb and saw that the stone had been removed from the tomb. So she ran and went to Simon Peter and the other disciple, the one whom Jesus loved, and said to them, "They have taken the Lord out of the tomb, and we do not know where they have laid him." Then Peter and the other disciple set out and went toward the tomb. The two were running together, but the other disciple outran Peter and reached the tomb first. He bent down to look in and saw the linen wrappings lying there, but he did not go in. Then Simon Peter came, following him, and went into the tomb. He saw the linen wrappings lying there, and the cloth that had been on Jesus' head, not lying with the linen wrappings but rolled up in a place by itself. Then the other disciple, who reached the tomb first, also went in, and he saw and believed; for as yet they did not understand the scripture, that he must rise from the dead.

- During 2006, two miners in Australia spent fourteen days trapped underground, facing slow death. After their rescue, their families and small community rejoiced as did their nation. People across the world followed their story.

- We are enthralled by such stories, about people who look disaster in the eye and make a new beginning. It is as though new life is granted to those who survive against such odds.

- Let me sit a while to contemplate the joy of the Easter story, of Jesus who lives, and who is present.